PRESENTED TO

_____

FROM

_____

DATE

_____

38 VALUES TO LIVE BY

All text originally appeared in *Life on the Edge* by James Dobson © 1995 by James Dobson. Word Publishing.

Unless otherwise indicated, Scripture quotations used in this book are from the King James Version of the Bible.

ISBN: 0-8499-1663-1

Printed in the United States of America

01 02 03 04 05 WOR 9 8 7 6 5 4 3 2 1

38
Values to Live By

Dr. James Dobson

INTRODUCTION

What drives our decisions in life? As individuals, we may be influenced by our families, our friends, or our environment, but the basis for the decisions we make can be reduced to one basic component: values. Whether they be lofty or lowly, noble or despicable, personal values are at the core of how we live.

In the pages that follow, I share thirty-eight principles that are the building blocks for a Christ-centered, abundant life. Through decades of counseling others and through my own experiences, I have seen these truths yield lifelong stability and spiritual prosperity.

What is it you seek? A deep and satisfying marriage? Meaningful friendships? Abiding faith? Learn these most basic values. Write them on your heart. Live by them. Your life will be richer for it.

38 Values to Live By

1

"Seek ye first the kingdom of God, and his righteousness; and all these things shall be added unto you" (Matthew 6:33). This is the fundamental principle of life on which all others rest.

2

TWO

BALA

One of the secrets

of successful

living is found in

the word "balance,"

the avoidance of harmful extremes.

38 Values to Live By

We need food,

but we should not overeat.

We should

work, but not

make work our

only activity.

We should play,

but not let play rule us.

38 Values to Live By

Throughout life,

it will be

important to

find the safety

of the middle ground

rather than the

imbalance of

the extremes.

3

THREE

*T*his is the way to be successful in life: Treat

every person as you want to be treated; look for

ways to meet the physical, emotional, and spiritual

needs of those around you. Suppress your desire to

be selfish and to seek unfair advantage over others.

38 Values to Live By

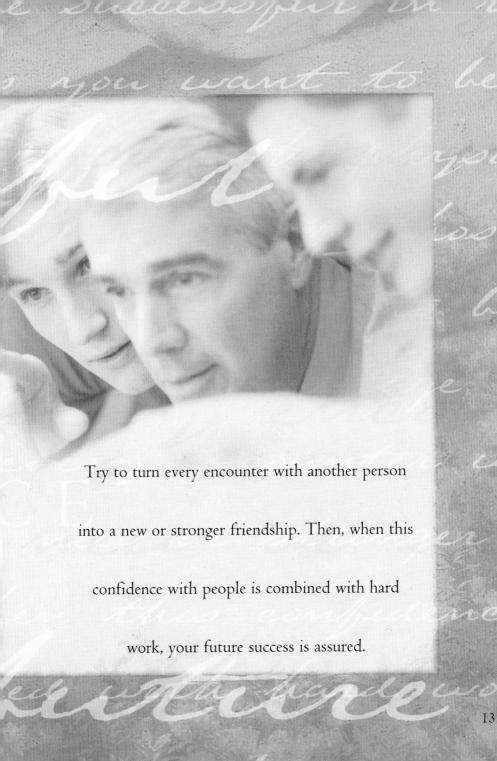

Try to turn every encounter with another person

into a new or stronger friendship. Then, when this

confidence with people is combined with hard

work, your future success is assured.

38 Values to Live By

FOUR

4

As a general

rule, don't risk

what you can't

afford to lose.

The overwhelming feeling of being "in love" is not a very reliable emotion during the early years—or at any age!

This intense

affection can

evaporate in a

matter of days,

leaving the

person confused

(and perhaps

unhappily married).

The only way to

know you are in love

with another

person is to give

yourself plenty of time

to get acquainted.

Once the decision

is made to marry,

your commitment to

one another will be much

more important than

your feelings, which are

certain to come and go.

38 Values to Live By

6

FEELINGS ARE

NEITHER RIGHT

NOR WRONG.

IT'S WHAT YOU

DO WITH THEM

THAT CAUSES

THE PROBLEMS.

7 *The universe and everything in*

38 Values to Live By

it will someday be made new by the Creator.

Therefore, the events

of today that

seem so important

are not really

very significant,

except those matters that

will survive the end of the universe.

*I*f you're going through difficult times, hold steady. It will change soon. If you're experiencing smooth sailing and easy times now, brace yourself. It will change soon. The only thing you can be certain of is change.

8

38 Values to Live By

NINE
9

*W*HENEVER TWO HUMAN BEINGS SPEND

TIME TOGETHER, SOONER OR LATER THEY

WILL PROBABLY IRRITATE ONE ANOTHER. THIS

IS TRUE OF BEST FRIENDS, MARRIED COUPLES,

PARENTS AND CHILDREN, OR TEACHERS AND

STUDENTS. THE QUESTION IS: HOW DO THEY

RESPOND WHEN FRICTION OCCURS?

THERE ARE FOUR BASIC WAYS THEY CAN REACT:

38 Values to Live By

1. *They can internalize anger*

and send it downward into a

memory bank that never forgets.

This creates great pressure within

and can even result in disease

and other problems.

2. They can pout and be rude without discussing the issues. This further irritates the other person and leaves him or her to draw his or her own conclusions about what the problem may be.

3. They can blow up and try to hurt the other person. This causes the death of friendships, marriages, homes, and businesses.

• Or, they can talk to one another about their feelings, being very careful not to attack the dignity and worth of the other person. This approach often leads to permanent and healthy relationships.

38 Values to Live By

*M*ost loneliness results from insulation rather than isolation. In other words, we are lonely because we insulate ourselves, not because others isolate us.

10

TEN

LATION

11

ELEVEN

*I*T IS

BETTER TO BE

SINGLE AND

UNHAPPY

THAN

UNHAPPILY

MARRIED.

38 Values to Live By

38 Values to Live By

TWELVE

12

Your life is before you. Be careful of the choices you make now that you could regret later. This regret is the subject of an old poem whose author has been forgotten. I hope you'll never have reason to apply it to yourself.

Across the fields of yesterday,

He sometimes comes to me

A little lad just back from play—

The boy I used to be.

He looks at me so wistfully

When once he's crept within;

It is as if he hoped to see

The man I might have been.

38 Values to Live By

38 Values to Live By

13

THIRTEEN

God is entitled to a portion of our income—not because He needs it, but because we need to give it.

14

FOURTEEN

"The love of money is

the root of all evil"

(I Timothy 6:10).

That's why Jesus issues

more warnings about

materialism and wealth

than any other sin.

Obviously, it takes a

steady hand to hold

a full cup.

38 Values to Live By

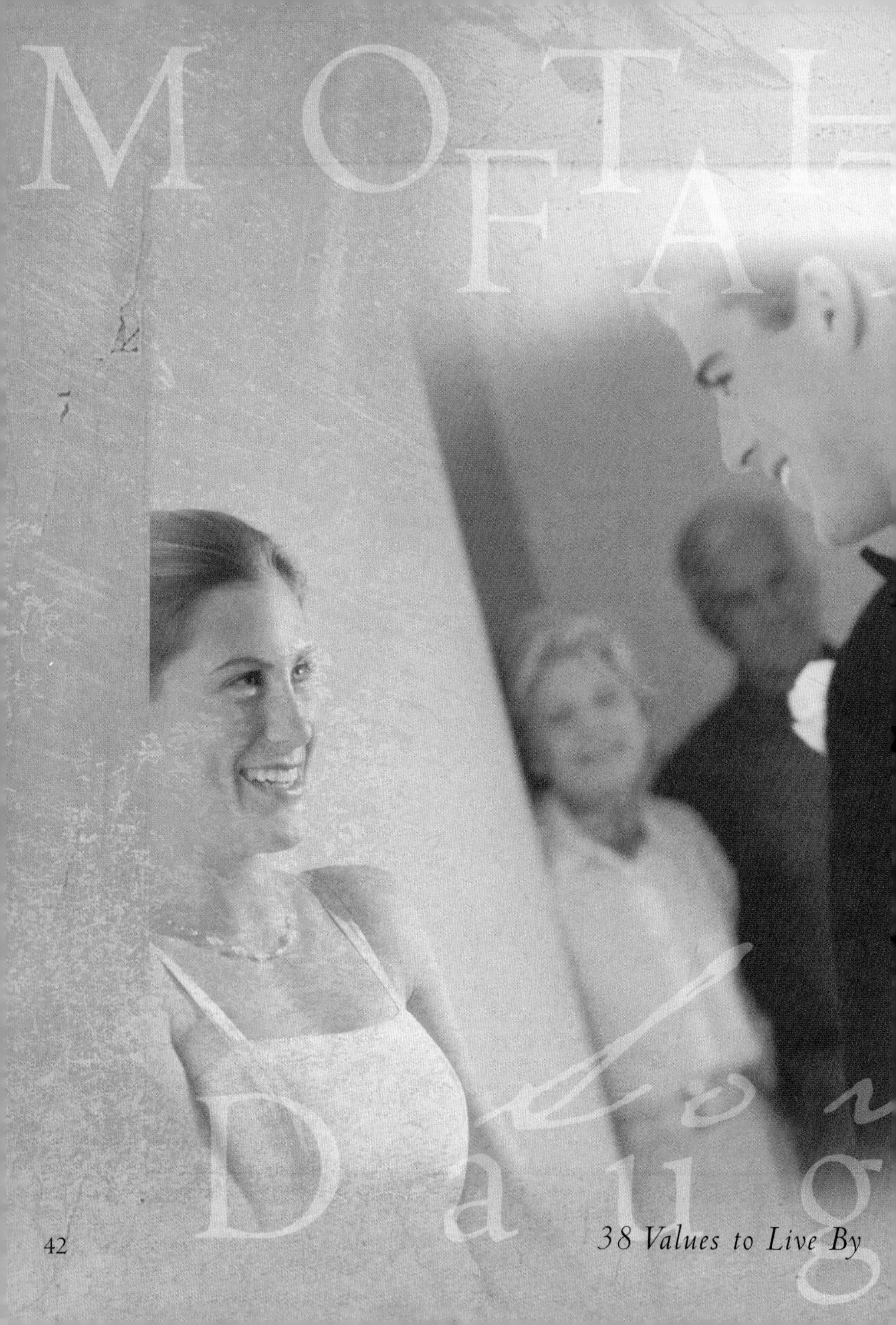

15

There will come a day when young people will want to move out and establish a home of their own—perhaps much sooner than their parents would wish.

After that time, a mother and

father will be more like friends

than parents. And someday,

if the parents live long enough,

their children will be more

like parents to them than

sons or daughters.

SIXTEEN

16

38 Values to Live By

Parenting is tougher than it looks. Before you criticize your parents for their failures and mistakes, ask yourself: Will I really do that much better with my own children?

S

38 Values to Live By

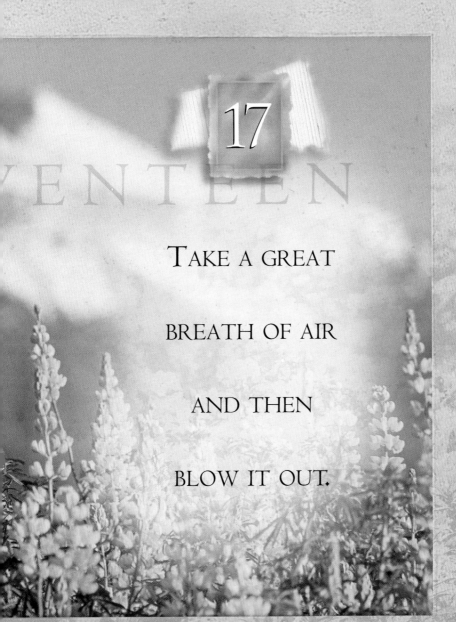

17

SEVENTEEN

TAKE A GREAT

BREATH OF AIR

AND THEN

BLOW IT OUT.

Contained in that single breath were at least three nitrogen atoms that were breathed by every human being who ever lived, including Jesus Christ, William Shakespeare, Winston Churchill, and every president of the United States. This illustrates the fact that everything we do affects other people, positively or negatively. That's why it is foolish to say, "Do your own thing if it doesn't hurt anybody else." Everything we do affects other people.

OUT. TAKE A GREAT BREATH OF AIR AND THEN

HEN BLOW IT OUT. TAKE A GREAT BREATH OF

A GREA

IT OUT

D THEN

ATH OF

A GREA

IT OUT

D THEN

ATH OF

friend

38 Values to Live By

*I*t takes time
to develop any friendship,
whether with a loved one
or with God Himself.
Overcommitment
and time pressure are
the greatest destroyers
of marriages and
families.

18

EIGHTEEN

God created two sexes, male and female. They are equal in worth, although each is unique and different. It is not only impossible to blend maleness and femaleness into a single sex, it is dangerous to even attempt it.

20

TWENTY

*T*HE ONE TRUE GOD *wants us to bring ou*

Values to Live By

eeds, problems, and decisions to Him. He has promised to lead us into all truth (see John 8:32). Therefore, Christians should never consult astrologers, psychics, or those who practice witchcraft (see Isaiah 47:13–14). They are usually phonies who only pretend to have extrasensory powers, and in some cases are working in cooperation with Satan.

21

*S*trong desire is like a river. As long as

it flows within the banks of God's will—

be the current strong or weak—all is well.

But when it overruns those boundaries and

seeks its own channels, then disaster lurks

in the rampage below.

—JAMES DOBSON, SR.

38 Values to Live By

22

TWENTY

TWO

With God,

even when nothing

is happening...

something is happening.

23

GOD GAVE U

38 Values to Live By

HUMAN WORTH

DOES NOT DEPEND

ON BEAUTY,

INTELLIGENCE, OR

ACCOMPLISHMENTS.

WE ARE ALL MORE

VALUABLE THAN THE

POSSESSIONS OF THE

ENTIRE WORLD SIMPLY

BECAUSE GOD GAVE US

THAT VALUE. THIS FACT

REMAINS TRUE, EVEN

IF EVERY OTHER PERSON

ON EARTH TREATS US

LIKE LOSERS.

24

TWENTY
FOUR

38 Values to Live By

The killing of unborn children through medical abortions is one of the most evil occurrences of our time, with 1.5 million babies sacrificed in America and 55 million worldwide each year.

TWENTY
FIVE

25

THE FIRST FIVE MINUTES OF EVERYTHIN

38 Values to Live By

ARE VITALLY IMPORTANT, ESPECIALLY TO:

A new friendship

A pastor's sermon

A family during the early-morning hours

A dad who has just come home from work

A television program

A salesman's presentation

A visit to the doctor.

38 Values *to Live By*

*T*hose first few moments of any human activity set the stage for everything that follows. If we begin our task properly, we will probably be successful over the long haul. Therefore, spend more time preparing for the first five minutes than any comparable period of time.

38 Values to Live By

38 Values to Live By

TWENTY SIX

'26

*R*emember, balance and moderation are needed in television watching, too. Some men watch so many sporting events on television that they wouldn't even know of their wives' decision to leave them unless it was announced on "Monday Night Football"!

God made each of us,

individually. Comparison

is the root of all feelings

of inferiority.

27

The moment you begin

examining other people's

strengths against your most

obvious weaknesses, your

self-esteem starts to crumble!

38 Values to Live By

28

GOD IS LIKE A FATHER TO
HIS CHILDREN. HE LOVES
THEM MORE THAN THEY
CAN UNDERSTAND, BUT HE
ALSO EXPECTS THEM TO BE
OBEDIENT TO HIS WILL. AND
HE HAS SAID, "THE WAGES OF
SIN IS DEATH" (ROMANS 6:23).
IT IS STILL TRUE.

29

*T*hose who are

the happiest are

not necessarily

those for whom

life has been

easiest.

*E*motional stability results from an attitude. It is refusing to yield to depression and fear, even when black clouds float overhead. It is improving that which can be improved and accepting that which is inevitable.

THIRTY

30

COMMUNISM AND SOCIALISM

are economic systems whereby the

government assumes responsibility

to see that each person's needs are met

and that no one individual earns more

than the state feels is fair.

CAPITALISM,

such as we have in

America, is based on

free enterprise, whereby

a person can achieve a

better income for himself

and his family by working

and sweating and saving

and investing.

38 Values to Live By

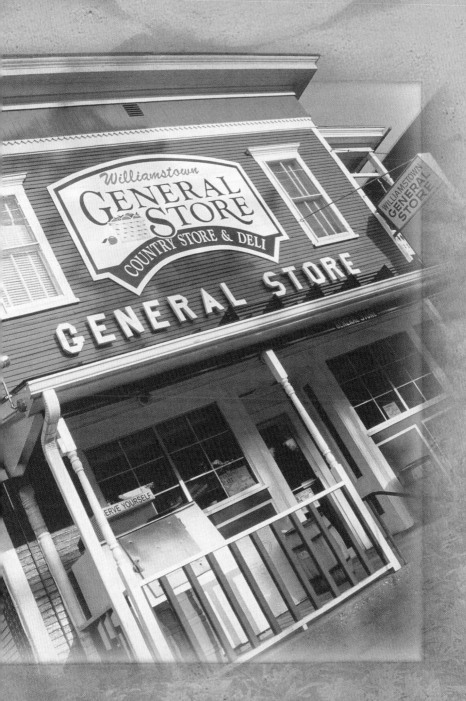

To compare these systems, think of yourself about to take a history test. Suppose you studied very hard and earned an A, but the teacher gave you a C so he could share some of your correct answers with a failing student who didn t study at all. Obviously this would destroy your motivation to study in the future.

*T*his need for personal incentives explains why capitalism produces more energetic people than communism and socialism, and why America is the richest nation on earth.

*The human body seems
indestructible when we
are young. However,
it is incredibly fragile
and must be cared for
if it is to serve us
for a lifetime. Too often,
the abuse it takes*

during early years
(from drugs,
improper nutrition,
sporting injuries, etc.)
becomes painful
handicaps in later years.

38 Values to Live By

32

THIRTY TWO

Sexual contact between a boy and a girl is a progressive thing. In other words, the amount of touching and caressing and kissing that occurs in the early days tends to increase as they become more familiar and at ease with each other. Likewise, the amount of contact necessary to excite each other increases day by day, leading in many cases to an ultimate act of sin and its inevitable consequence.

*T*his progression must be consciously resisted by Christian young people who want to serve God and live by His standards. They can resist this trend by placing deliberate controls on the physical aspect of their relationship, right from the first date.

38 Values to Live By

SATAN WILL ATTEMPT TO OFFER YOU WHATEVER YOU HUNGER FOR, WHETHER IT BE MONEY, POWER, SEX, OR PRESTIGE. BUT JESUS SAID, "BLESSED ARE THOSE WHO HUNGER AND THIRST FOR RIGHTEOUSNESS" (MATTHEW 5:6).

33

34

"Except the Lord
build a house,
they labour in
vain that build it"

(PSALM 127:1).

38 Values to Live By

38 Values to Live By

35

*D*on't marry someone with intolerable characteristics in the hopes of changing him or her. If you can't live with someone who drinks or someone who isn't a Christian or someone who isn't clean, then don't marry that kind of person. The chances of miraculous improvements or changes in behavior are slim. What you see is what you get!

36

*F*aith in God is like

believing a man can walk over

Niagara Falls on a tightrope

while pushing a wheelbarrow.

Trust in God is like getting

in the wheelbarrow!

38 Values to Live By

N GOD

38 Values to Live By

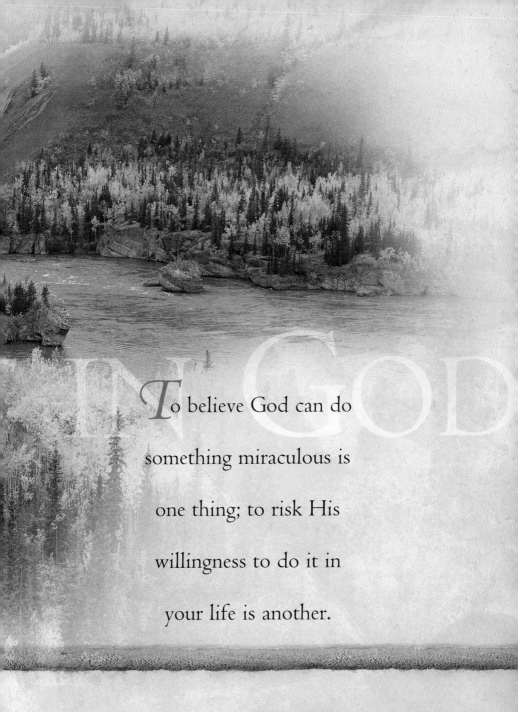

*T*o believe God can do

something miraculous is

one thing; to risk His

willingness to do it in

your life is another.

"A wet bird never

38 Values to Live By

37

flies at night."

(My grandfather said that to me

when I was a child and warned

me not to forget it. I remember

his words but never did figure

out what he meant!)

38

"*For* what shall it profit

a man if he shall gain

the whole world, and lose

his own soul?"

(JESUS' WORDS IN MARK 8:36).

38 Values to Live By

Other Books
by DR. JAMES DOBSON

Children at Risk (with Gary L. Bauer)

Coming Home

Emotions: Can You Trust Them?

Home with a Heart

In the Arms of God

Life on the Edge

Love for a Lifetime

Love Must Be Tough

Parenting Isn't for Cowards

Preparing for Adolescence

Solid Answers

Stories of the Heart and Home

Straight Talk to Men

The New Dare to Discipline

The New Hide or Seek

The Strong-Willed Child

What Wives Wish Their Husbands Knew about Women

When God Doesn't Make Sense